Taking on Water

poems by

Ellen McNeal

Finishing Line Press
Georgetown, Kentucky

Taking on Water

Copyright © 2012 by **Ellen McNeal**
ISBN 978-1-62229-032-1 First Edition
All rights reserved under International and Pan-American Copyright Conventions. No part of this book may be reproduced in any manner whatsoever without written permission from the publisher, except in the case of brief quotations embodied in critical articles and reviews.

ACKNOWLEDGMENTS

"If You Don't Mind" appeared in The Comstock Review Spring/Summer 2010 Edition

Editor: Christen Kincaid

Cover Art: Ellen McNeal

Author Photo: Welton and Karen Becket

Printed in the USA on acid-free paper.
Order online: www.finishinglinepress.com
also available on amazon.com

Author inquiries and mail orders:
Finishing Line Press
P. O. Box 1626
Georgetown, Kentucky 40324
U. S. A.

TABLE OF CONTENTS

The Runner	3
I Shall Not Want	4
Delivered	5
Promise	6
Once Removed	7
Water	8
With a Vengeance	9
Borne	10
Don't Call	11
Pinioned	12
Overwhelmed	13
Cast	14
This	15
I Swear	16
Mother of Sons	17
Secrets	18
If You Don't Mind	19
This Matters	20

The poems in this collection are written from vocabularies taken from the biblical Book of Psalms.

The Runner

A cup on the table,
my daily walk over,
I dwell on before,
when I ran paths
with my shadow
following my lead,
ahead of my past.

For the sake of a good life,
a good run.
I was fearless,
restored.

A cup on the table,
my daily walk over,
I could lie down
in this comfortable house,
and I'd still
be out
running the past.

I shall not want

They lie in shadowy paths,
on the run – copperheads, rattlers.
I'm not prepared for snakes
near the house.
What I want is comfort:
green valleys, still water, and pastures
to walk, a full cup on the table,
the good life I lead.

So, I get out my sickle,
hack down what remains
of lantana, hibiscus, mexican heather.
I cut to the ground, disturb
honeybees, hummingbirds, victims
themselves of an old fear that raises
its merciless head. Oh, lord, all for the sake
of my comfort, the good life restored.

Delivered

A thousand birds would know me   We'd nap in green folds of the hills

I'd eat fruits of the forest   I could get high without mountains

be filled without drink   Fruit of my flesh

I'd glorify mornings   I'd refuse all your troublesome calls

fly with the birds   Rid of the beast

    I'd be wild outrageously me

Promise

Of course,
this was uttered
in night speech
language
of lovers and moons
circuitous rooms
of the sleepless

nightlines and endlines
running on nothing
everything waiting
edgy
a bridegroom

Once Removed

              So,
we pitied ourselves,
gone from that place.
As children, we framed
all our days in fields of high grass
and flowers, a west wind upon us.

Passing among us, our father,
who was known as a man
of great kindness, loved us more than
this earth, and without fear,
we flourished.

        But I've digressed,
and winds shift by day to the east. Once
removed, I knew the dust of remember
and when.

Water

has taken his breath
and his noise

taken play from this house
and song from her harp

death as our host
still faithful we gather

songs from her harp
play from this house

noise of our own
breath   taking on water

With a Vengeance

she washes burned pots,
working in silence,
judging her hands
and the breakage,
speeches and lies.

She was the voice
in men's ears,
a whirlwind, the sun
before sons, blood
of their births.

She lets water pass
through her teeth, over
her hands, cuts on her feet.
Deaf to the runoff,
wizened, estranged.

Borne

You're more needy
now than I, together
borne as one.

Words you speak
double cross your tongue,
your lips, my heart.

You sigh *poor me*,

and I walk
a solitary walk,
wish you better, wish

you here,
silver-spooned,
reborn.

Don't Call

when you've been drinking
or when you're high.

I can tell
by your uneven speech.

Your mountains of trouble
needn't be mine.

I've sacrificed worlds
and offered reprovals.

You know the beast's
in your blood.

Hear me out, don't
bullishly pay with your flesh.

Vow not to drink;
call me.

Pinioned

by night
he sees with his hands
wills falls to trust
unrewarded

Days are a snare
the waste of an arrow
noon
a refuge for flies

Fortress for bucklers
dark's day under cover
delivered in shadow
complacent

Overwhelmed

a broken man swallows

his name; given sides,

he snares

had beens and gone

overs again. Prey,

his escape's a rose

between teeth; help,

a bird sold

on upstream.

Cast

potsherds and bones

to the dogs, tongues

at their feet

when raving

and roars

pour from their jaws.

Stare down the bulls,

dust off your garments,

pull wax from your hands,

water your heart.

This

So much is true -
I was warned and worried
more than I would tell.
This becomes reward
for harboring regret,
holding back. Bearing loss,
I'd trade by night
the honeyed life I sought.

Bitter, I've become a servant to the comb,

the honeyed life I sought
I'd trade by night
holding back, bearing loss
for harboring regret.
Then *this* becomes reward,
more than I would tell.
I was warned and worried,
just so much is true.

I Swear

we could live in the woods,
        share a big house, rest
                from our work in the fields.

One at a time, you could sit
        on this stool, I'd teach you again
            the secret

        of tying your shoes, which
                foot the left, which the right
                turn to take.

You'd lie down at night;
        I'd watch the arc of the sky, the slightest
            affliction of eyelids,
                every disturbance of sleep.

Clothed in moonlight,
        I'd look at your faces…children.
                Remember. Call home.

Mother of Sons

Who knows the number
of years. Will it be
three or four, maybe ten?

How soon before sorrow
works its way in?

Do me a favor:
concerning the children,
be glad they've returned.

Glorify mornings
with kindness and reason.

All of you do me a favor:
forget what's due
and evening the score.

Don't be so proud.
Once more let me see you
hold hands.

Secrets

       follow me
precede me
a shadow of myself

I cover my eyes
           let
                them
                      fall

fill my hands

           let
        them
    fall

I close my eyes

a shadow of myself
precedes me
     follows secrets

If You Don't Mind

I'll consider the sea

set out with fish

lick my fingers and feet

What if I choose to

work among oxen in fields

no man has ordained

or make paths on a full moon

by myself

too close to stars

graze with the sheep

I'd oversee things with birds

if I want

    there will be options

This Matters

Speaking with grace,
a ride in the fall.
Writing your thigh.
Children
and hands
and the truth.

Arrows
and tongues,
men fallen from glory
on terrible speeches.
Memory,
things
we forget.

Ellen McNeal is a poet and a weaver. Her poetry has appeared in ARACHNE: HANGING BY A THREAD; THE COMSTOCK REVIEW; UP COUNTRY; SEASONS; PASSAGER; THE PEN WOMAN; HAPPY BIRTHDAY, MR. LINCOLN; TOWER POETRY, and ART TIMES.

She has received awards for her writing from The Chautauqua County Council on the Arts and The National League of American Pen Women. Her poems have won 1st place in the Abacus and Rose Poetry Contest, from the Canastota, New York Library Poetry Competition, and Honorable Mention in the 2004 Milton Dorfman Poetry Prize Contest, sponsored by the Rome Art and Community Center. Her haiku have won awards from Syr-Haiku Poetry Contest and from the Syracuse Poster Project. In 2005 her poem *Les Fauves* won 2nd prize in the Milton Dorfman Poetry Contest. Some of her poems have recently been acquired by MUSC (Medical University of South Carolina) as part of their Art/Poetry Project. She is a 2009 nominee for the Pushcart Prize.

Ellen is the author of A FRIEZE DRAWN OVER PEACE, a chapbook of ghazals and woodscapes. She has served as Editor of SEASONS, a literary quarterly, and is currently an Associate Poetry Editor of THE COMSTOCK REVIEW.